SO-Ell-354

HERE IT'S WINTER

Kathleen Beal

1. Here it's win-ter, here it's win-ter, with snow and sleds. Here it's win-ter, here it's win-ter, with snow and sleds and co-zy beds. Here it's win-ter, here it's win-ter, with snow and sleds and co-zy beds. Wear___ your___ hat! But in South A-mer-i-ca, it's sum-mer.___ Think of that!

Music by Dwight Beal

A Publication of the World Language Division

Project Director: Elinor Chamas
Editorial Development: Elly Schottman
Production/Manufacturing: James W. Gibbons
Design/Art Direction: Joanna Fabris
Illustrator: Paige Billin-Frye

Copyright © 1991 by Addison-Wesley Publishing Company, Inc. All rights reserved. No part of this publication may be reproduced, stored in a retrieval system, or transmitted in any form or by any means, electronic, mechanical, photocopying, recording, or otherwise, without the prior written permission of the publisher. Printed in the United States of America.

ISBN 0-201-52208-X
2 3 4 5 6 7 8 9 10—WZ—95 94 93 92 91

▲▼ Addison-Wesley Publishing Company
Reading, Massachusetts • Menlo Park, California • New York • Don Mills, Ontario
Wokingham, England • Amsterdam • Bonn • Sydney • Singapore • Tokyo • Madrid • San Juan

Here it's winter,
Here it's winter,
With snow and sleds.

Here it's winter,
Here it's winter,
With snow and sleds
And cozy beds.

Here it's winter,
Here it's winter,
With snow and sleds
And cozy beds.
Wear your hat!

But in South America,
It's summer.

Think of that!

Here it's spring,
Here it's spring,
With melting snow.

Here it's spring,
Here it's spring,
With melting snow
And buds that grow.

Here it's spring,
Here it's spring,
With melting snow
And buds that grow.
Get your ball and bat!

But in South America,
It's fall.

Think of that!

Here it's summer,
Here it's summer,
Take a hike.

Here it's summer,
Here it's summer,
Take a hike
Or ride your bike.

Here it's summer,
Here it's summer,
Take a hike
Or ride your bike.
Jump KERSPLAT!

But in South America,
It's winter.

Think of that!

Here it's fall,
Here it's fall,
With books to take.

Here it's fall,
Here it's fall,
With books to take
And leaves to rake.

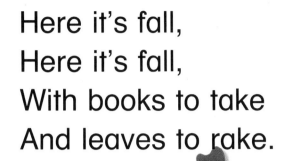

Here it's fall,
Here it's fall,
With books to take
And leaves to rake.
Squirrels get fat.

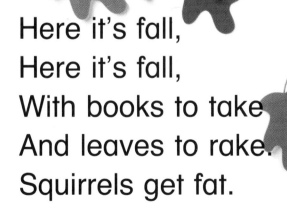

But in South America.
It's spring.

Think of that!